LEARN TO DRAW

Disney PRINCESS

Enchanted Princesses

Learn to draw Ariel, Cinderella, Belle, Rapunzel, and all of your favorite Disney princesses!

Illustrated by The Disney Storybook Artists

Table of Contents

Tools & Materials

You'll need only a few supplies to create all of your favorite Disney princesses. You may prefer working with a drawing pencil to begin with, and it's always a good idea to have a pencil sharpener and an eraser nearby. When you've finished drawing, you can add color with felt-tip markers, colored pencils, watercolors, or acrylic paint. The choice is yours!

drawing pencil & paper

eraser

sharpener

colored pencils

felt-tip markers

paintbrushes & paints

How to Use This Book

In this book you'll learn to draw your favorite princesses in just a few simple steps. You'll also get lots of helpful tips and useful information from Disney artists that will guide you through the drawing process. With a little practice, you'll soon be producing successful drawings of your own!

First draw the basic shapes using light lines that will be easy to erase.

Each new step is shown in blue, so you'll know what to draw next.

Follow the blue lines to draw the details.

Now darken the lines you want to keep, and erase the rest.

Use some magic (or crayons or markers) to add color to your drawing!

Snow White

Even when she's abandoned in the forest, Snow White's kindness shines through and wins her the friendship of all the forest animals—as well as the love and loyalty of the Seven Dwarfs. When you draw Snow White, be sure to show the soft, sweeping lines in her dress and the gentle arm movements that emphasize her cheerful, sweet disposition and her joy for life.

NO! not too curvy

lines are graceful

NO! not angular

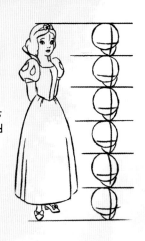

Snow White is about 6 heads tall

figure is rounded

5

6

hands are rounded and soft . . .

. . . not sharp and pointed

draw the legs as a guide, even though they're covered by skirt

YES! skirt is wider than hips

feet are small and delicate

7

Cinderella

Cinderella's beauty and graceful movements are evident as she runs down the stairs in her simple, homemade gown, but they are even more obvious at the ball. When she first arrives in her gorgeous dress (thanks to her Fairy Godmother), she immediately attracts everyone's attention, including Prince Charming's. When you draw her sweeping gown with billowing curves, show just a bit of the elegant lace underneath.

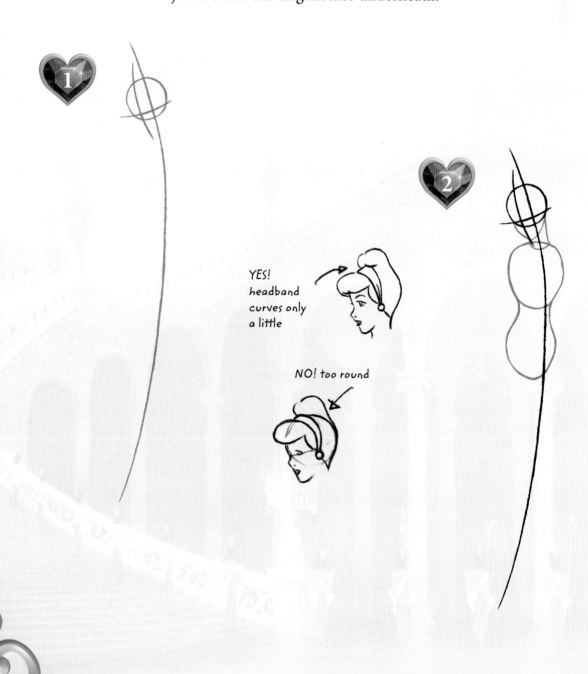

YES! headband curves only a little

NO! too round

3

Cinderella is about 6-1/2 heads tall

4

YES! Cinderella's waist is full but not too plump

NO! waist is not so thin

5

headband is straighter on top than on side

6

Cinderella's fingers are long and slender

YES! angles are soft and smooth

NO! angles are not sharp

7

Sleeping Beauty

When Aurora is awakened from her sleep by a kiss from Prince Phillip, she is saved from the curse placed upon her at birth—and she gets to marry her true love! Now when she dances with her prince in the palace, her simple dress is exchanged for a lovely gown, and a beautiful tiara replaces her plain headband. Use long, slightly curved lines for her skirt to show how regal this princess has become.

eyes tilt up slightly

top of head is
fairly flat

Sleeping Beauty's
features are more
angular than
Snow White's or
Cinderella's

 YES! eyes end in
pointed corners
and have one
thick eyelash

 NO! not round—
don't draw
individual lashes

Sleeping Beauty
is about 6-1/2
heads tall

waist is
very slim

Sleeping Beauty's
hair curls like this
at the back

YES! Sleeping Beauty's hair extends behind head at an angle

NO! not straight down the back of head

large bangs on left

big curl on right

YES! curls are closed, like this

NO! not open curls

when she dances, hair swings out like this

Ariel

People around the world have been charmed by Ariel's cheerful enthusiasm. Be sure to show some of her energy when drawing her complete figure.

Ariel is about 6-1/2 heads tall from the top of her hair to the tip of her fins

Ariel's body curves more behind . . .

. . . and curves less in front

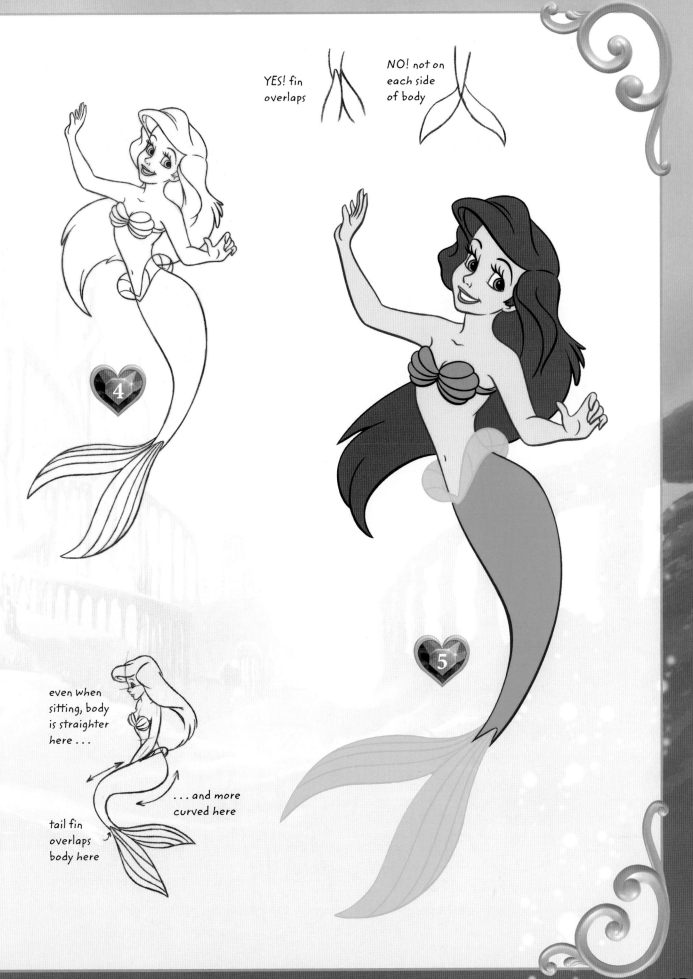

YES! fin overlaps

NO! not on each side of body

even when sitting, body is straighter here . . .

. . . and more curved here

tail fin overlaps body here

Belle

Belle radiates kindness and love in her elegant ball gown.

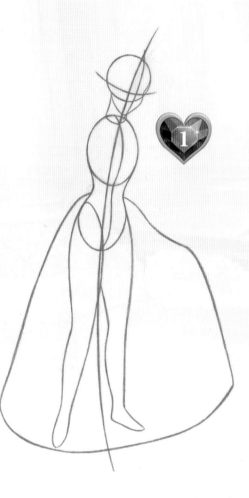

when worn down, Belle's hair is drawn with simple shapes that wrap around her head

YES! hair curves around head

NO! no straight line across head

Belle is about 6¹/₂ heads tall

in ponytail, hair
is pulled close
to head

Jasmine

Jasmine has a slender figure. She carries herself with dignity and grace.

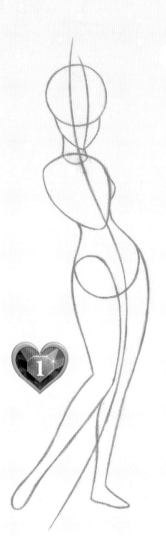

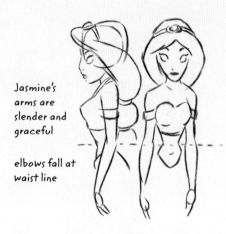

Jasmine's arms are slender and graceful

elbows fall at waist line

1

2

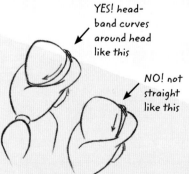

YES! head-band curves around head like this

NO! not straight like this

Jasmine is
just a little
more than
5 heads tall

Pocahontas

Pocahontas's body is athletic yet feminine. She stands with her shoulders back and her head held high.

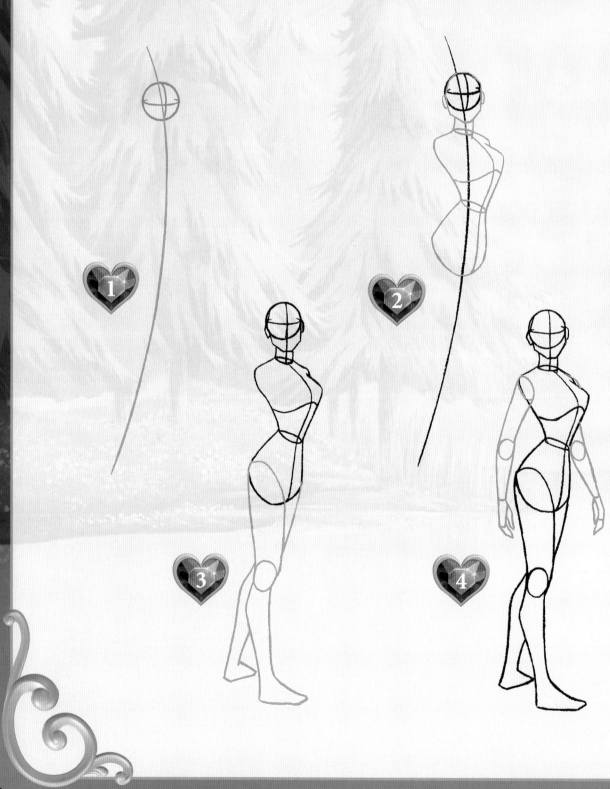

Mulan

This plucky heroine is a study in contrasts. Mulan is graceful, yet feisty; respectful, yet defiant. Behind her classic Asian features lies a quick mind—and she's not afraid to speak it. Animators had to show both the outwardly traditional Mulan and her bold inner spirit. They chose to create her character using simple shapes and few details. Her clean, down-to-earth look emphasizes that she just wants to be true to herself. As you draw Mulan, focus on simplicity, shape, and proportion.

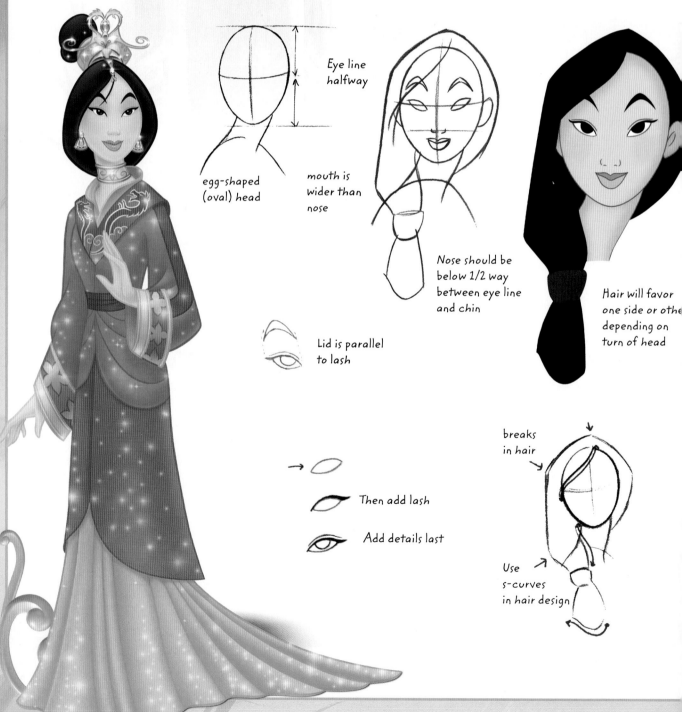

Eye line halfway

egg-shaped (oval) head

mouth is wider than nose

Nose should be below 1/2 way between eye line and chin

Lid is parallel to lash

Then add lash

Add details last

Hair will favor one side or other depending on turn of head

breaks in hair

Use s-curves in hair design

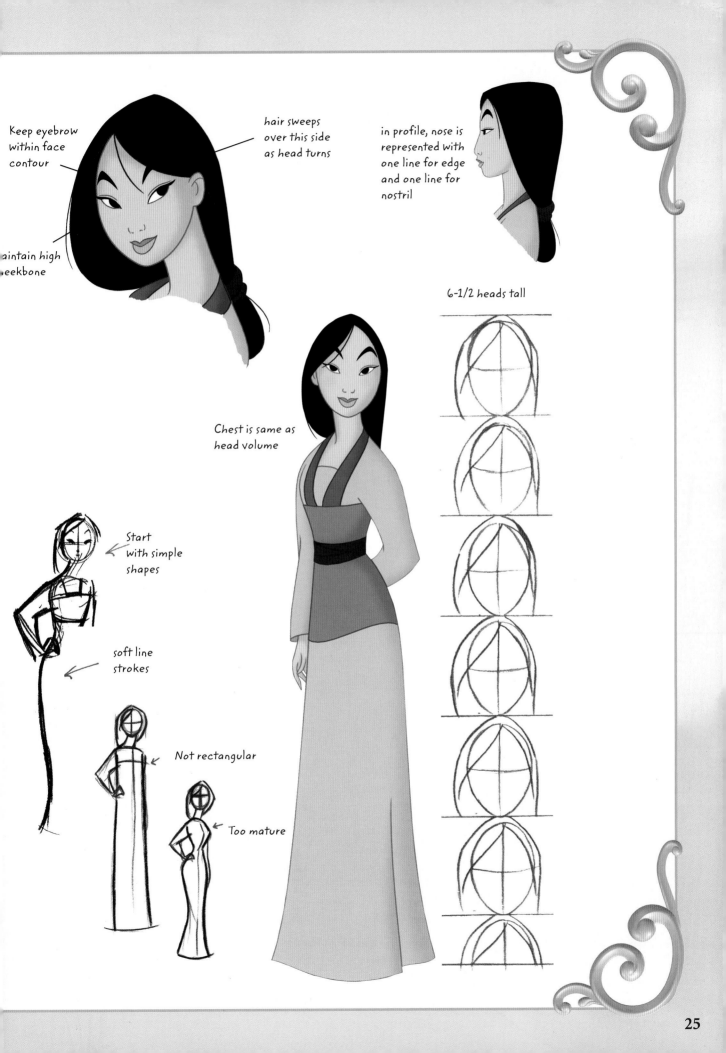

Keep eyebrow within face contour

hair sweeps over this side as head turns

in profile, nose is represented with one line for edge and one line for nostril

aintain high eekbone

6-1/2 heads tall

Chest is same as head volume

Start with simple shapes

soft line strokes

Not rectangular

Too mature

Mulan as Soldier

Mulan becomes a soldier to save her elderly father's life. She defies tradition, doing what she believes is right. The film's artists have followed her daring lead and treated her "soldier" look with an unconventional approach. Her basic features are the same, but slight changes have been made to help hide her femininity. Here are some secrets to drawing Mulan as a soldier:

Widow's peak

Hair is closer to head when pulled back

Ears stick out prominently

Lips are slightly less curvy than on "normal" Mulan and are natural in color

Slightly smaller eyes; eye has no "tail" lash or lid indication like "normal" Mulan eyes

Slightly angled-out jawline

Even when she is in armor, retain Mulan's graceful shapes

Show some thickness of hair

S-curve shallow bridge

Eye close to nose

slight overbite

Watch space here

NO!
Too wide

Too small

Tiana

When Tiana marries Naveen, she not only regains her human form, she becomes a princess! Tiana finally gets her dream restaurant and finds true love with her prince!

Tiana has dimples on her cheeks

nose is about same width as the distance between eyes

narrow wrists

full bottom lip

Tiana's bayou wedding crown is made of petals and stamens of varying shapes and sizes

Rapunzel

Rapunzel may have grown up in a tower, but she is full of energy, which she uses to take care of her hair that grew and grew and grew! Her days are full of many things, including reading, cooking, and painting. Her beautiful art covers the walls (and the ceiling!) of the tower. When drawing Rapunzel, don't forget to think of her spirit and her curiosity about the world outside. Even though she could not leave the tower, she dreamed big!

the "swoop" at the top of Rapunzel's hair is a distinguishing feature of her look

NO!

YES!

hair has volume
and thickness, even when
lying on the floor

Rapunzel's
hair has a lot
of weight that
forms simple
shapes

Conclusion

Now that you've learned the secrets to drawing your favorite Disney princesses, try creating different scenes from the movies, or original scenes of your very own. To create a little magic, all you need is a piece of paper, a pencil, and your imagination!